GRAMMAR SKILLS

Grades 2—3

by Rachel Gordon, Toni Jones and Rosemary Allen

Published by World Teachers Press®

Nouns   Parts of Speech   Adverbs
Plural Forms
Comparatives and Superlatives
Verb Tenses   Irregular Verbs
Imperatives   Conjunctions   Homophones
Questions   Punctuation   Adjectives
Irregular Plurals

Order Number 2-5127
ISBN 1-58324-051-9

C D E F 03 02

Educational Resources
395 Main Street
Rowley, MA 01969
www.worldteacherspress.com

Over the years, controversy about the value of teaching grammar concepts to students has challenged teachers and, to some degree, led to an uncertainty in this area of the curriculum. However, there has been a resurgence of interest in grammar and a recognition of the need for teachers and students to share a common language which allows them to talk about language and how it operates as a resource for making meaning.

This three book series has been written in response to this need: to provide teachers with a practical teaching resource that can add to their knowledge of how the English language functions and how it is organized to serve those functions. It recognizes that basic to any teacher's effort to help students improve their grammar is the teacher's own understanding of how the English language works.

English grammar should not be something you dread teaching. It is merely what teachers have been doing for years. The terminology is slightly different, but by using familiar and understandable text, it can be comfortable for your students to grasp.

Grammar Skills is about using "real text" to understand and experiment with "real language." Students have an innate sense of interest in stories that portray heroes and villains and that personify animals. Nursery rhymes, myths, legends, fairytales and fables will interest your students and bring them into the natural rhythm, flow, rhyme and picturesque language of the text. By using these genres which appeal to young minds, this book enables you to introduce the structure of language through text that is appealing.

Detailed teachers notes have been included throughout the book and the answer pages, providing explanations and additional activity ideas where appropriate.

Contents

Section 1 — Nursery Rhymes

Nursery Rhymes provide students with familiar text to begin to develop an understanding of grammar. This section of the book is broken down into distinct sections each containing the rhyme, history, a detailed explanation of each support activity and extension activities. Blackline masters are supplied to develop basic skills in various aspects of the English language.

Section 2 — Fairytales, Legends, Fables and Myths

Fairytales, legends, fables and myths is a section of this book that takes a more advanced look at the English language. This section utilizes student knowledge of popular stories to develop understanding and skills in English grammar. More complex areas of grammar are introduced and explored through basic activities.

Contents

Section 3 — Grammar

This section, covering nouns, adverbs and verb tenses, deals with grammar in a more formal situation and leads to the format for the following two books in the Grammar Skills series. Each area requires students to develop an understanding of the topic and explain the rules in their own words. This is an excellent strategy to encourage ownership of understanding and generally means students will remember and use their knowledge in a more successful manner.

Grammar Skills Teachers Notes

Teachers Notes and Answers

At the back of each book in the *Grammar Skills* series are detailed teachers notes and answers. These notes provide background information on the specific grammar concepts being studied and answers where required.

Section 1 — Nursery Rhymes

Generic pages have been included and can be used with any story in Section 1 or with other stories being dealt with in the classroom. The following pages are provided:

Basic English Grammar — 1 page 8

Basic English Grammar — 2 page 9

The worksheets in this book are suitable for use with large or small groups. It is recommended that a copy be enlarged to use in discussion.

The rhymes used in the book should be read and discussed prior to completing the worksheets so students can focus on the structure of the language used.

Words of the rhyme are supplied.

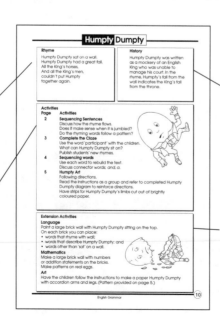

Background information is given to explain the derivation of the rhyme.

Activities are explained page by page. Ideas for discussion or presentation of activities are included.

Extension activities for other subject areas are provided.

Grammar Skills | Teachers Notes

Section 2 — Fairytales, Legends, Fables and Myths

Generic pages have been included and can be used with any story in Section 2 or with other stories being dealt with in the classroom. The following pages are provided:

The worksheets in this book are suitable for use with large or small groups. The fairytales, legends, fables and myths used in the book should be read and discussed prior to completing the worksheets so students can focus on the structure of the language used. The activities introduce basic grammar concepts as outlined in the Table of Contents.

Section 3 — Grammar

This section begins to introduce formal grammar concepts, focusing on nouns, adverbs and verb tenses. *Grammar Skills 4–5* and *6–8* follow this format. Activities are presented in a variety of ways allowing students to develop a level of interest and understanding of the content.

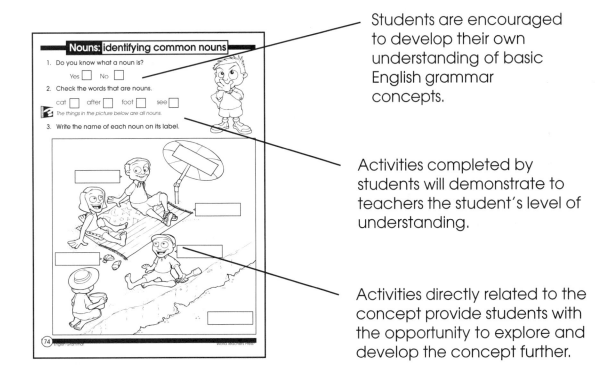

Students are encouraged to develop their own understanding of basic English grammar concepts.

Activities completed by students will demonstrate to teachers the student's level of understanding.

Activities directly related to the concept provide students with the opportunity to explore and develop the concept further.

These words can be introduced easily to young students. You will find they can use the terminology with confidence.

Participants – people and objects we find in the rhymes.

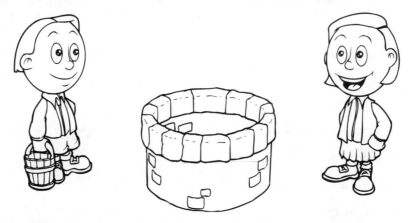

Processes – the actions in the rhymes.

Circumstances – where, why, when and how the characters function.

Students can make their own word walls as you find participants and processes in the rhymes.

✄ -

Humpty Dumpty

Rhyme

Humpty Dumpty sat on a wall.
Humpty Dumpty had a great fall.
All the King's horses,
and all the King's men,
couldn't put Humpty
together again.

History

Humpty Dumpty was written as a mockery of an English king who was unable to manage his court. In the rhyme, Humpty's fall from the wall indicates the king's fall from the throne.

Activities

Page	Activities
11	**Sequencing Sentences** Discuss how the rhyme flows. Does it make sense when it is jumbled? Do the rhyming words follow a pattern?
12	**Complete the Cloze** Use the word "participant" with the students. What can Humpty Dumpty sit on? Publish students' new rhymes.
13	**Sequencing Words** Use each word to rebuild the text. Discuss connector words, *and, a.*
14	**Humpty Art** Following directions. Read the instructions as a group and refer to completed Humpty Dumpty diagram to reinforce directions. Have strips for Humpty Dumpty's limbs cut out of brightly colored paper.

Extension Activities

Language

Paint a large brick wall with Humpty Dumpty sitting on the top.
On each brick you can place:
• words that rhyme with wall,
• words that describe Humpty Dumpty, and
• words other than "sat" on a wall.

Mathematics

Make a large brick wall with numbers or addition statements on the bricks.
Make patterns on real eggs.

Sequencing Sentences

1. Cut along the dotted lines.

2. Put the strips in order.

3. Glue onto a piece of paper.

Humpty Dumpty sat on a wall.

and all the King's men,

Humpty Dumpty had a great fall.

couldn't put Humpty together again.

All the King's horses,

1. Make your own rhyme.
2. Fill in the spaces with your own words.

_____   _____

sat on a wall.

_____   _____

had a great fall.

All the _____   _____

and all the _____   _____,

couldn't put _____

together again.

1. Cut along the dotted lines.
2. Put the words in order.
3. Glue onto a piece of paper.

fall.	men,	wall.	again.
horses,	All	together	the
on	King's	great	King's
the	Humpty	couldn't	put
sat	Dumpty	Humpty	all
and	a	Humpty	had
a	Dumpty	**Dumpty**	**Humpty**

1. Color the Humpty Dumpty parts.
2. Cut along the dotted lines.
3. Collect four strips of paper (2 cm wide, 12 cm long).
4. Fold accordion style. These are Humpty's arms and legs.
5. Glue arms to Humpty Dumpty's body. Glue hands.
6. Glue legs to Humpty Dumpty's body. Glue feet.

Jack and Jill

Rhyme

Jack and Jill went up the hill
to fetch a pail of water.
Jack fell down and broke his crown
and Jill came tumbling after.
Up Jack got and home did trot
as fast as he could caper.
He went to bed to mend his head
with vinegar and brown paper.

History

It is believed the rhyme is based on an old Scandinavian legend about two children who fetch water from the well. The moon scoops them up and carries them away as they tumble down the hill.

Activities

Page	Activities
16	**Complete the Cloze** Use the word "participant" with the students. What could be fetched? Publish students' new rhymes.
17	**"er" as in "caper" and "paper"** Word patterns. In *Grammar Skills* we encourage students to look at words and their use.
18	**Sequence the Story** Look at the beginning, middle and end of the rhyme in detail. What happens when the rhyme is jumbled?
19	**Complete the Cloze** The text gives us clues to the word that fits. This is a vital aspect of using semantics for reading.

Extension Activities

Language
Look at the vocabulary. What does "crown" mean? What does "caper" mean? List as many words as you can that also mean "trot."

Mathematics
Go outside for water play.
Compare tall containers with wide containers.
Look at volume. Does the color of the container affect how much each container can hold? Use two ice-cream containers of the same size but in different colors. Have water races carrying buckets of water.
Use a stopwatch.

Art
Go outside and let the students paint with water.
Water shows up on brick and concrete surfaces.

Complete the Cloze

1. Make your own rhyme.
2. Fill in the spaces with your own words.

_____ and _____

went up the hill

to fetch a _____

of _____ .

_____ fell down

and broke _____ crown

and _____ came tumbling after.

1. Circle the objects that end in "er."

2. Write as many words as you can that end in "er."

1. Color the pictures.
2. Cut along the dotted lines.
3. Put the pictures in order.
4. Glue onto a piece of paper.

to fetch a pail of water.

Jack fell down and broke his crown

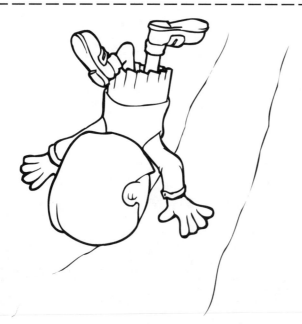

and Jill came tumbling after.

Jack and Jill went up the hill

Complete the Cloze

Write the correct word in the space to finish the cloze.

water	went	and	a	his	Jill	fell	crown

Jack _____ Jill

_____ up the hill

to fetch _____ pail of _____.

Jack _____ down,

and broke _____ _____

and _____ came tumbling after.

 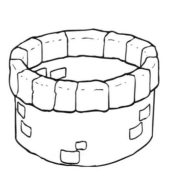 

Hey Diddle Diddle

Rhyme
Hey diddle diddle,
the cat and the fiddle,
the cow jumped over the moon.
The little dog laughed,
to see such sport
and the dish ran away with the spoon.

History
This is probably the most well known nonsense verse. It was first printed in 1765. There are many myths as to what it is about. One source claims that it refers to various constellations.

Activities

Page	Activities
21	**Complete the Cloze** Discuss the missing text. Are the "participants" missing? What about the word "see"? What is it?
22	**Where is the Cow?** Change the circumstance. Children change the circumstance in the rhyme. For example, the cow "jumped over a car" or "slid over the snow."
23	**Read and Draw** Illustrate and sequence. Discuss the importance of illustrations to support text.
24	**The Dog Said ...** Discuss the mode of the text. The mode or model is written text. When would you have spoken text? For example, in a phone conversation or on the playground. Have the students write what the dog would say to the dish.

Extension Activities

Language
Discuss different types of string instruments.
Write words that rhyme with "diddle."

Mathematics
Measure the distance that each student can jump.
Record each student's result.
Graph the results.

Drama
Act out the story as one student reads the rhyme.

Complete the Cloze

Write the correct word in each space to finish the cloze.

cat	cow	spoon	fiddle	dog	moon

Hey diddle diddle,

the _____ and the _____,

the _____ jumped over

the _____.

The little _____ laughed

to see such sport,

and the dish ran away with

the _____.

1. Finish this sentence. Write a different place the cow might go.

Hey diddle diddle,

the cat and the fiddle,

the cow _____

_____ .

2. Draw a picture to show where the cow went.

1. Read the sentences.
2. Color the pictures.
3. Cut along the dotted lines.
4. Put the pictures in order.
5. Glue onto a piece of paper.

The little dog laughed,
to see such sport,

Hey diddle diddle,
the cat and the fiddle,

the cow jumped over
the moon.

and the dish ran away
with the spoon.

1. Write what the dog might say to the dish.
2. Color the picture.

I'm a Little Teapot

Rhyme
I'm a little teapot
short and stout.
Here is my handle,
here is my spout.
When I get all steamed up,
then I shout,
"Tip me over and pour me out!"

History
Many people think this is a nursery rhyme. However, it is only a chant.

Activities

Page	Activities
26	**Fill the Teapot** Fill in the missing text. Look at the pronouns (I, me, my).
27	**Complete the Cloze** Change the pronouns by adding a new participant. Discuss that participants can be a person's name or something like "I," "me," or "my," rather than using the term "pronoun" with young students.

Extension Activities

Language
Look at different types of tea leaves.
Describe the feel and smell of each one.

Mathematics
How many cups fill a teapot?
How many teapots does it take to fill a bucket?

Art
Design a teapot.
Make a prototype from recycled materials.

Fill the Teapot

1. Read the words in the box next to the teapot.
2. Read the rhyme.
3. Write the words in the spaces to finish the rhyme.

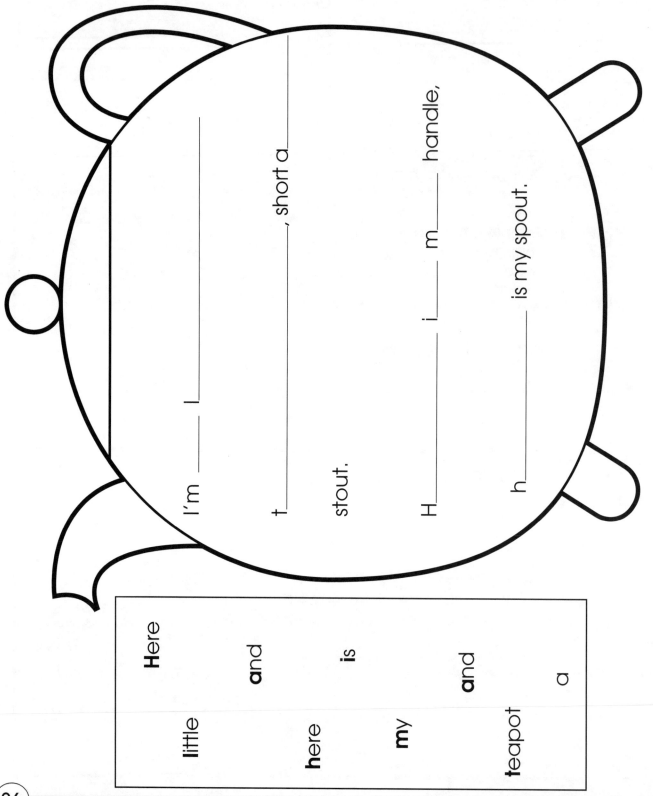

I'm _____ l_____, short a
t_____
stout.
H_____ i_____ m_____ handle,
h_____ is my spout.

Here   little

and   here

is   my

and
teapot

a

Write Your Own

1. Make your own rhyme.
2. Use your name to fill the first space.
3. Finish the rhyme by filling in the spaces.

_____ is a little teapot,

short and stout.

Here is _____ handle,

here is _____ spout.

When _____ gets all steamed up,

then _____ shouts,

"Tip _____ over and pour _____ out!"

Little Miss Muffet

Rhyme
Little Miss Muffet,
sat on a tuffet,
eating her curds and whey.
Along came a spider,
which sat down beside her,
and frightened Miss Muffet away.

History
It is believed that at the end of the sixteenth century Patience Muffet was born. Her father was an entomologist (a person who studies insects). Needless to say, there were many spiders, bugs and crawly critters around the house. Some sources say that one day she was frightened by a ferocious spider. However, some sources say the rhyme was simply to make fun of her eccentric father.

Activities

Page	Activities
29	**Sequence the Story** Cut and sequence. Look at the beginning, middle and end of the rhyme in detail. What happens if the rhyme is jumbled?
30	**Write Your Own** Change the "participants." The students can participate in the rhyme by adding their own name.
31	**Changing Words** Look at inflections. Discuss the words "eating" and "sat" (sit, sitting, sat).

Extension Activities

Language
Look at the different versions of the rhyme:
• there came a big spider;
• along came a spider.
What is a "tuffet"? Depending on cultural backgrounds, some people will say it is a small stool with three legs and some people will say it is a mound of grass. Compare various illustrations and you will see that not all illustrators use the same item.

Mathematics
How far did Miss Muffet jump from her tuffet? Let the students measure the distance they can jump. Graph their results on a large chart.

Art
Make spiders using black stockings.
Add eight accordion legs.

Sequence the Story

1. Color the pictures.
2. Number the boxes in order.
3. Cut along the dotted lines.
4. Put the pictures in order.
5. Glue onto a piece of paper.

_____ ittle

_____ iss

_____ uffet

Write Your Own

1. Finish the rhyme.
2. Use your name to fill the first space.
3. Finish the rhyme by filling in the spaces.

Little _____,

sat on a _____,

eating _____ _____ and

_____.

Along came a _____,

which sat down beside _____,

and frightened

_____ away.

World Teachers Press®

1. Underline the words that have been changed.

Little Miss Muffet

was sitting on her tuffet.

She ate her curds and whey.

2. Write the words here.

_____

_____

3. Draw the spider.

Mary, Mary Quite Contrary

Rhyme

Mary, Mary quite contrary
How does your garden grow?
With silver bells and cockleshells
and pretty maids all in a row.

History

It is speculated that Mary, Queen of Scots, had a beautiful dress with silver bells and cockleshells. The pretty maids were four ladies that served her royal needs.

Activities

Page	Activities
33	**Interviewing Mary** Discuss the use of question marks. Brainstorm the questions you could ask Mary about her garden.
34	**Sequencing Sentences** Restructure the text. Discuss how the rhyme flows. Does it make sense when it is jumbled? Do the rhyming words follow a pattern?

Extension Activities

Mathematics

Make a large flower with a number in the middle. Students fill each petal with a statement that has an answer that matches the number in the middle.

Studies of Society and Environment

Discuss royalty.
What is a queen?
Discuss the environment and what we need to do to preserve our beautiful gardens.

Science

Plant some seeds and chart the rate of growth.
Place a white carnation in water with dark food color. Discuss how food travels up the stem of the flower. Watch the flower change color.

Art

Make a floral garden for Mary using colorful crepe paper.
Make large tissue flowers. Use five pieces of square tissue and lay them on top of one another. Fold like a fan and tie around the middle. Pull each layer up towards the middle to form the petals.

World Teachers Press®

1. Pretend you are Mary.
Read the questions.
Draw your answers.

(a) What kind of flowers do you like?

(b) What do you give your plants to help them grow?

(c) What color are the cockleshells in your garden?

Sequencing Sentences

1. Cut along the dotted lines.

2. Put the lines in order.

3. Glue onto a piece of paper.

How does your garden grow?

Mary, Mary, quite contrary

and pretty maids all in a row.

With silver bells and cockleshells

Mary Had a Little Lamb

Rhyme

Mary had a little lamb,
its fleece was white as snow.
And everywhere that Mary went,
the lamb was sure to go.

It followed her to school one day,
that was against the rule.
It made the children laugh and play,
to see a lamb at school.

History

There are conflicting reports about who really wrote this fabulous rhyme. There are two "Marys" who claim to have written it. Sarah Hale of Boston published the poem in 1830. However, Mary Tyler claimed the poem was written by John Ralston and she was the original Mary. The mystery still remains.

Activities

Page	Activities
36	**Fill the Lamb** Fill in the missing text. Use beginning sounds. The sheet has the words at the bottom of the page to accommodate a lower skill level.
37	**Finish the Rhyme** Write in the "participants." Discuss the simile "white as snow" and help students create a new one.
38	**Sequencing Sentences** Restructure the text. Discuss a variety of textual clues. Look at the first word in each line, point at each word, look at the first letter.

Extension Activities

Language
Look at similes:
• "white as snow," "black as coal," "green as grass"

Mathematics
Use the lamb outline on page 36 with the words deleted. Put large blocks inside the lamb to see what area the lamb holds.

Science
Visit a farm and look at the life cycle of a sheep.

Art
Make fluffy lambs with cotton balls.

Drama
Act out the rhyme in the playground.

Fill the Lamb

1. Read the words at the bottom of the lamb.
2. Read the rhyme.
3. Fill in the spaces to finish the rhyme.

Mary h _____ a l _____ lamb,

its fleece w _____ white a _____ snow.

A _____ everywhere t _____ Mary w _____

t _____ lamb w _____ sure t _____ g _____ .

was	as	go	that	had
the	little	to	And	went

1. Fill in the spaces to finish the rhyme.

_____ had a little _____,

Its _____

was _____ as _____.

And everywhere that _____ went,

the _____ was sure to go.

2. Draw a picture to show the rhyme.

Sequencing Sentences

1. Cut along the dotted lines.

2. Put the lines in order.

3. Glue onto a piece of paper.

Mary Had a Little Lamb

its fleece was white as snow.

Mary had a little lamb,

the lamb was sure to go.

And everywhere that Mary went

World Teachers Press®

Old Mother Hubbard

Rhyme
Old Mother Hubbard
went to the cupboard,
to fetch her poor dog a bone.
But when she went there,
the cupboard was bare,
and so the poor dog had none.

History
Old Mother Hubbard actually has 14 verses! It was written by Sarah Katherine Martin in 1804. Old Mother Hubbard was actually her brother's housekeeper. The rhyme was written just for fun.

Activities

Page	Activities
40	**Finish the Rhyme** Change the "process." Students should find it easy to talk about the process. Try to use the word in natural circumstances. For example, Old Mother Hubbard could run, walk or jump to the cupboard.
41	**The Dog Said ...** A look at speech bubbles. Discuss how you can make a character speak.

Extension Activities

Language
Look at vocabulary.
What does "fetch" mean?
Use words to describe Mother Hubbard.

Mathematics
Each child makes a paper cupboard.
Fill the cupboard with arbitrary bone shapes.
How many will fit?
Graph who does and does not own a dog.

Studies of Society and Environment
Discuss pet care.

Art
Use a real "doggy treat" bone to print designs.
It will give a fantastic bone shape!
Make a large collage of Old Mother Hubbard.

Finish the Rhyme

1. Read the rhyme.

2. Write words in the spaces to finish the rhyme.

Old Mother Hubbard

_____ to the cupboard,

to _____ her poor dog a bone.

But when she _____ there,

the cupboard was bare,

and so the poor dog had none.

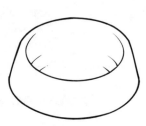

3. Draw Old Mother Hubbard looking into a bare cupboard.

Write what the dog would say when the cupboard was bare.

Little Jack Horner

Rhyme

Little Jack Horner,
sat in the corner,
eating his pudding and pie.
He put in his thumb,
and pulled out a plum,
and said, "What a good boy am I!"

History

Little Jack Horner was a real person. He was given a pie to take to the King in London. He became suspicious about this strange cargo and had a peek under the crust. He took out one of the select properties to keep for himself — the plum. He told the King it was his reward for delivering the pie safely.

Activities

Page	Activities
43	**Finish the Sentence** Look at direct speech. Look at the quotation marks to see what Jack actually said. Have the students write what they would say (clever girl, great boy).
44	**Finish the Rhyme** Discuss and give Jack some new actions.

Extension Activities

Language
Look at words that end in "er," Horner, corner.
Discuss quotation marks — who is speaking in the rhyme?

Mathematics
Talk about symmetry.
Is a pie a symmetrical shape?
Find other foods that are symmetrical.
Talk about halves, quarters and one whole.

Art
Use berries as natural dyes to paint with.

Cooking
Make your own fruit pie.

Finish the Sentence

1. Draw a picture of yourself with the pie.

2. Finish the sentence with what you would say.

"What a _____

_____ am I!"

1. Read the rhyme.

2. Write words in the spaces to finish the rhyme.

Little Jack Horner,

_____ in the corner,

_____ his pudding and pie.

He _____ in his thumb,

and _____ out a plum,

and said, "What a good boy am I!"

Hot Cross Buns

Rhyme
Hot cross buns, hot cross buns!
One a penny, two a penny,
hot cross buns.
If you have no daughters,
give them to your sons!
One a penny, two a penny,
hot cross buns.

History
This was an old chant that those who were selling hot cross buns would shout in the streets. The seventeenth and eighteenth centuries were when these sellers were frequently seen selling buns on the streets.

Activities

Page	Activities
46	**Exciting Words** Exclamations! Discuss what an exclamation mark is and when you would use it. Refer to the history of the rhyme to explain how it indicates the speaker is shouting.
47	**Word Search** Letters are put together in a particular way to form words.

Extension Activities

Language
Research the history of the hot cross bun. What does the cross symbolize?

Mathematics
Display the old currency and discuss the different system we use today. Make some rubbings of old coins.

Cooking
Cook some hot cross buns.

Exciting Words

1. Write seven words that express excitement. Remember the exclamation mark (!).
2. Color the clouds.

great!

Word Search

1. Find the following words.

buns	daughter	to	your
give	sons	hot	one
them	cross		

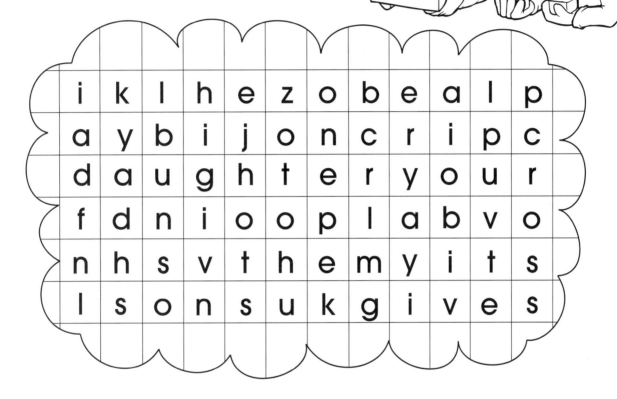

i	k	l	h	e	z	o	b	e	a	l	p
a	y	b	i	j	o	n	c	r	i	p	c
d	a	u	g	h	t	e	r	y	o	u	r
f	d	n	i	o	o	p	l	a	b	v	o
n	h	s	v	t	h	e	m	y	i	t	s
l	s	o	n	s	u	k	g	i	v	e	s

2. Write the words in alphabetical order.

_____

_____

_____

_____

Story Evaluation

1. Title of the story _____

2. Main character _____

3. Other important characters _____

_____

4. Was there a hero? ☐ Yes ☐ No

If yes, who was it? _____

5. Was there a villain or a bad character? ☐ Yes ☐ No

If yes, who was it? _____

6. How many different events happened in the story? _____

7. Was there a problem in the story? ☐ Yes ☐ No

If yes, what was it? _____

_____

8. Was there a solution to the problem? ☐ Yes ☐ No

9. Was there a lesson learned from the story? ☐ Yes ☐ No

If yes, what was it? _____

My Thoughts About the Story

1. What I liked _____

_____

_____

_____

2. What I did not like _____

_____

_____

_____

3. My favorite character _____

4. What I thought about the ending _____

_____

_____

Character Profile

Choose a character from your story and complete the profile.

Character

Strengths

Weaknesses

Likes

Dislikes

Physical Characteristics

Who is Speaking?

1. Read the story below.
2. Use a green pencil to underline where Papa Bear is speaking.
3. Use a red pencil to underline where Baby Bear is speaking.

Baby Bear looked up and said, "Someone's been sitting in my chair." He began to cry. Mama Bear said, "Someone's been in my chair too!" Papa Bear roared, "Someone's been sitting in my chair and I'm not happy!" The three bears went into the dining room. As Papa Bear started to sit down at the table he noticed a dirty spoon by his bowl. "Who's been eating my porridge?" Papa Bear shouted.

4. Here are some words from the story:
   cry, roared, shouted, not happy, looked up.
   Match the words to the character.

Baby Bear	Papa Bear
_____	_____
_____	_____
_____	_____
_____	_____

Add an Adverb

Words that tell **where**, **when** or **how** have been left out of this story. Complete the story with adverbs.

Little Goldilocks ran _____ through the forest.
(how)

She saw a tiny cottage and went _____. She loved
(where)

what she saw! She opened the door and went straight to the

table. She _____ gobbled up the breakfast that was
(how)

_____. She _____ rummaged
(where)   (how)

through the house. She decided to take a quick nap. That was

when the bear family came home. They _____ looked
(how)

around the house for a stranger!

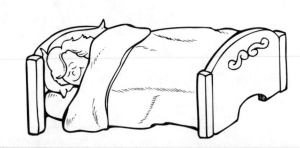

They found Goldilocks!

Exclamation Marks

1. An exclamation mark is used to show excitement, anger or surprise. Make this statement show anger.

Someone's been sitting in my chair.

_____

_____

2. Make this question into a statement that shows surprise. You can add more words.

Who's been sleeping in my soft bed?

_____

_____

3. Change the mood and write your own statement.

Baby Bear said, "_____

_____."

Papa Bear said, "_____

_____."

Cut out the connecting words at the bottom of the page and use them to connect the sentence parts below.

Jack climbed up the beanstalk

[ ] went into the

castle. He heard the giant's big feet stomping

[ ] he wasn't scared! He was in the kitchen

[ ] he decided to hide in the oven!

Jack stole the giant's hen [ ] he fell asleep.

The giant woke [ ] chased Jack!

| and | but | when | so | and |

Make it Connect

In the story below the connecting words are written in bold.
Complete the story.

Jack saw the giant. **However,** _____

_____ .

He loved the giant's gold **and** _____ .

In addition, he loved _____ .

While the giant was _____

_____ .

Jack stole the _____

_____ .

The giant woke up **so** Jack had to _____

_____ .

Storymap

Start at Jack and map what happened along the road.

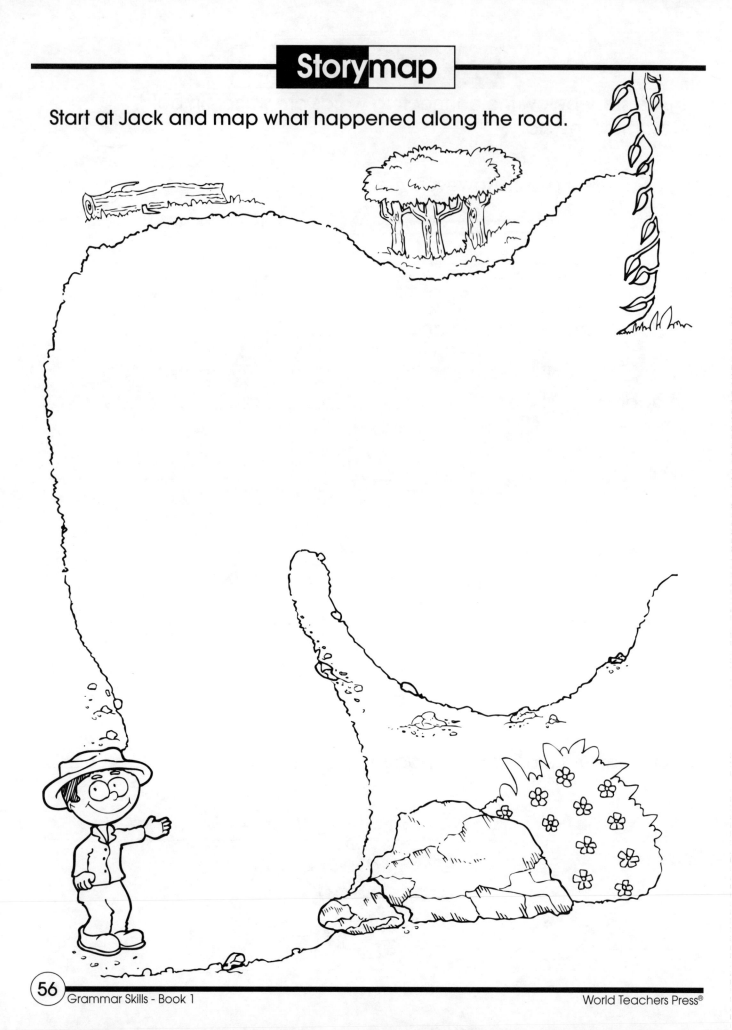

Word Bank

A noun group is a group of words that describes a person, place or thing. For example, "The third fat little pig" or "A little house of sticks." Write some noun groups you might find in the story of the Three Little Pigs.

Change the Mood of the Wolf

1. Compare a traditional version of the story of the three pigs to a newer version.

(a) Is the mood different in each one? _____

(b) How is the wolf different in the newer version?

_____

2. Find some lines to compare the mood.

Old version	New version
Little Pig, little pig, let me in!	_____
Or I'll huff and I'll puff ...	_____
_____	_____
_____	_____
_____	_____

Using Words that Describe

1. Describe the wolf.

_____

_____

2. Describe Little Red Riding Hood.

_____

_____

3. Describe Grandma's house.

_____

_____

4. Check the words that could be used to describe the following.

house   ☐ clever   ☐ brick   ☐ small   ☐ sad

horse   ☐ green   ☐ fast   ☐ hungry   ☐ big

ocean   ☐ rough   ☐ happy   ☐ blue   ☐ smooth

apple   ☐ red   ☐ tall   ☐ shiny   ☐ crunchy

Character Profile

1. Write as many words as you can about King Arthur under each heading.

King Arthur

(a) Friends

(b) Enemies

(c) Strengths

(d) Weaknesses

(e) Favorite Things

1. Read the sentences below,
   then fill in the spaces.

Arthur became King when he

_____ the sword from the stone.

_____ had a _____ called Camelot.

King _____ and the knights would sit

_____ a great round table and plan their

adventures. He _____ a great leader.

2. Make different words using the letters from this statement.
   King Arthur and the Round Table.

Cut the strips apart and arrange them so they tell about King Arthur.

King Arthur

and plan their adventures.

Arthur became King when

King Arthur and the knights

he pulled the sword from

the stone.

would sit around a great round table

The Ducks and the Fox

Cut the strips and arrange them so they tell about the ducks and the fox.

On their way they met a fox sitting on a fence.

Two duck sisters were waddling down the road to the pond for a swim.

"Oh yes," said the sisters, "we come along here every day."

The next morning the first sister said, "I think we should take another road to the pond."

"Good morning, ladies," said the fox. "Are you on your way to the pond?"

"No," said the second sister. "I am used to this road." So off they went along the same road.

"Interesting," said the fox, with a toothy smile. "Have a nice swim."

Up ahead the fox was waiting and tried to catch the duck sisters. They were able to get away but decided they would not take the same road every time.

Using Pronouns

1. **Complete the story below using pronouns where possible.**

The two ducks were waddling down the road when

_____ met a fox sitting on the fence.

_____ was smiling. _____ told Fox

_____ walked that way every morning. The next

day _____ was waiting with a sack.

_____ jumped on _____ and flew home.

The ducks found a new way to walk the next time they went out.

2. **List some pronouns below.**

_____ _____

_____ _____

_____ _____

_____

Talking Ducks

1. In the spaces, write what the ducks said about the lesson they learned.

2. Write the conversation below.

(a) The first duck said, "_____

_____

_____,"

(b) The second duck said, "_____

_____

_____."

The Baboon's Umbrella

Cut the strips and arrange them so they tell about the baboon's umbrella.

"My good friend," said the gibbon, "how strange to find you holding an open umbrella over your head on such a sunny day as this."

The baboon was taking his daily walk in the jungle. He met his friend, the gibbon, on the path.

"There is a simple solution," said the gibbon. "You need only to cut some holes in your umbrella. Then the sun will shine on you."

"Yes," said the baboon. "I am most annoyed. I cannot lose this disagreeable umbrella. I am stuck. I would not think of walking without my umbrella in case it should rain."

"But, as you see, I am not able to enjoy the sunshine underneath this dark shadow. It is sad."

In the end the baboon got soaked to the skin.

"What a good idea!" The baboon went home and cut holes in his umbrella.

World Teachers Press®

Procedure — Umbrella Repair

Write a procedure to tell how to repair an umbrella that has had holes in it.
What could someone do to fix it?
What materials would they need? Remember that a procedure is simply instructions telling someone how to do something!

1. Answer the questions below about how to fix an umbrella.

(a) What is your goal?

_____

_____

_____

_____

(b) What materials will be needed?

_____

_____

_____

(c) What steps need to be followed?

_____

_____

_____

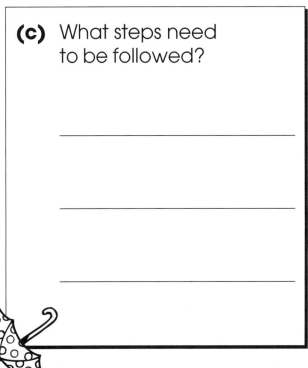

2. Use the information above to write your procedure.

1. Write some adjectives to describe what would make a good umbrella.

2. Design an umbrella.

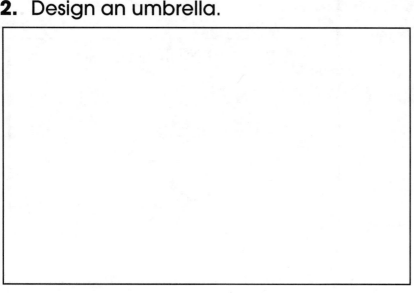

3. Write an advertisement for your umbrella. Use some interesting adjectives.

Zeus Complete the Cloze

1. Use the words in the box below to complete the cloze.

| was | made | lied | thunderbolt | the | hurled |

Zeus was a supreme ruler of the gods.

Zeus _____ a powerful god. He was lord of

_____ sky. His weapon was a _____

and he _____ it at people who

_____ him angry.

Zeus punished people who _____.

2. Finish these sentences.

(a) Zeus was a _____

_____.

(b) Zeus did not like _____

_____.

Zeus Character Profile

1. Write words to describe Zeus in the correct spaces.

(a) Bad deeds

(b) Good deeds

(c) Strengths

(d) Weaknesses

(e) Physical features

2. Illustrate Zeus on another piece of paper.

Processes for Zeus

1. List as many processes as you can that tell about Zeus.
Some have been done for you.

Mental processes	Material processes
thinks *wonders*	*yells* *fights*

2. List the material processes that you do. Try to list six.

_____ _____ _____

_____ _____ _____

3. List the mental processes that you do.
Try to list six.

_____ _____

_____ _____

Compare Yourself to Zeus

Compare yourself to Zeus and complete the table below.

	Me	Zeus
Physical Appearance		
Strengths		
Weaknesses		
Likes		
Dislikes		

1. Write a report on another mythological god. Use this planning sheet to collect your information. You will need to use books or the computer to help you with your research.

   (a) Name of god

   _____

   (b) Where he or she lived

   _____

   _____

   (c) Special powers

   _____

   _____

   (d) What he or she looked like

   _____

   _____

   (e) Other notes

   _____

   _____

2. Write your report on another piece of paper, but first try to write your opening sentence below.

   _____

   _____

1. Do you know what a noun is?

Yes ☐   No ☐

2. Check the words that are nouns.

cat ☐   after ☐   foot ☐   see ☐

The things in the picture below are all nouns.

3. Write the name of each noun on its label.

Nouns: classifying common nouns

Do you know what a noun is now?
A noun is the name of something.

1. Write some nouns that have to do with transportation.

_____   _____   _____

_____   _____   _____

_____   _____   _____

2. Write some nouns that have to do with kitchens.

_____   _____   _____

_____   _____   _____

_____   _____   _____

3. Write some nouns that have to do with school.

_____   _____   _____

_____   _____   _____

_____   _____   _____

4. Write some nouns that have to do with sport.

_____   _____   _____

_____   _____   _____

1. Look at the pictures. Write one word to describe what you see.

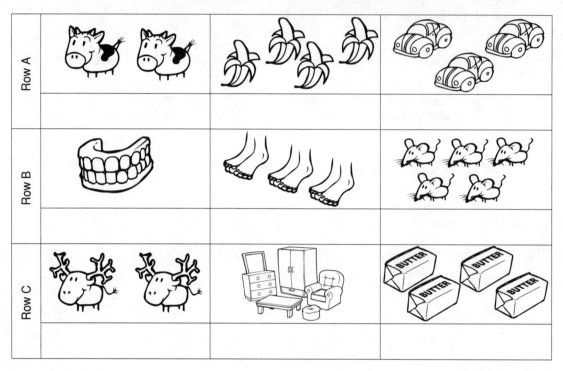

The words you have written are all plurals. Rows A and B have countable nouns in them. Row C has uncountable nouns in it.

2. Use the pictures as clues to answer the following questions.

What is a plural? _____

What is the difference between the nouns in Row A, Row B and Row C?

Row A _____

_____

Row B _____

_____

Row C _____

_____

Nouns: plural spelling rules

 Some plurals are easy because they are made the same way.

1. Write the singular form next to each plural and write how the plurals are made.

    (a) girls _____   cats _____

    mountains _____ hats _____

    (b) How are these plurals made?

    _____

2. **(a)** beaches _____   wishes _____

    ashes _____   boxes _____

    bunches _____

    branches _____

    brushes _____   taxes _____

    (b) How are these plurals made?

    _____

3. **(a)** parties _____   stories _____

    armies _____

    (b) How are these plurals made?

    _____

Nouns: irregular plurals

You have already learned some ways to make plurals. Here are some sentence pairs that have missing plurals. These are different from the ones you used before. Parts of the word must change to make the plural.

1. Complete these sentences.

(a) My baby has a tooth. Really? My baby has four _____.

(b) Look at that man over there.

Which man? I can see three _____.

(c) A goose swam in the small pond.

Five _____ swam in the big pond.

(d) A mouse just ran across the floor.

There must be a nest of _____ somewhere.

(e) My foot hurts from walking on the hard road.

You're lucky. Both of my _____ hurt.

(f) The woman next door is very kind.

Most of the _____ in this street are kind.

(g) My eldest child likes to go to the movies on the weekends.

All of my _____ like movies.

Sometimes we use other words to help make plurals.

2. Complete these sentences.

(a) Only a _____ people ordered coffee but

_____ people ordered tea.

(b) Add a _____ sugar to the pie.

World Teachers Press®

Adverbs: telling how

1. Read this story.

> The alarm clock rang **loudly**. Mother opened the door **quietly** and shook Madison **gently** until she was awake. "Come on, sleepyhead. The sun is shining **brightly** and your father is waiting **patiently** to take you to the zoo."
>
> Madison climbed out of bed **sleepily**, yawned and went into the bathroom to have a shower. She dressed **quickly** and ran down stairs **happily**. She knew she would have fun at the zoo.

2. Look at the words in bold print. In what way are they alike?

_____

The words in bold print have a special name. They are called adverbs because they add more meaning to the verb in the sentence. They tell "how." Loudly tells how the alarm clock rang. Quietly tells how mother opened the door.

3. Complete the following.

(a) Gently tells _____

(b) Brightly tells _____

(c) Patiently tells _____

(d) Sleepily tells _____

(e) Quickly tells _____

(f) Happily tells _____

4. Here are some verbs. Add an adverb that tells more about the verb.

(a) laughed _____   **(b)** snored _____

(c) snored _____   **(d)** ran _____

(e) banged _____   **(f)** crawled _____

Adverbs: that tell frequency and time

 You know about verbs that tell "how" — some adverbs tell more about "when" and "how often."

1. Read this story.

A Lesson for Lee

Lee loved art. More than anything he wanted to win the school art prize. His mother reminded him **daily** to begin his drawing, but he **never** listened to the advice. "You are **always** late," said his mother. "You will be sorry one day."

"It will be a holiday soon. I'll do it then," promised Lee.

The holiday came and Lee worked all day on his drawing. He was pleased with all his drawings, but one was his best.

With this drawing I'm sure to win, he thought. It was very good. However, he forgot to take it to school the next day.

Two days went by before he carefully wrapped the drawing and gave it to his teacher. "Here is my entry for tomorrow, Miss Lee."

"Tomorrow?" Miss Lee shook her head. "You are too late, Lee.

Entries closed yesterday. I can't accept it today. You should have put it in earlier."

From that day on, Lee was always early. He had learned his lesson.

 Look at the adverbs in bold print. They are adverbs that tell "when" and "how often."

2. Can you find more adverbs in the story? Draw a line under them.

3. Use adverbs of frequency to write about yourself.

(a) Tell about something you always do.

_____

(b) Tell about something you never do. _____

_____

(c) Tell about something you often do. _____

_____

(d) Tell about something you rarely do. _____

 World Teachers Press®

Some words are useful if you want to describe something to another person. Here is an example.

Linda woke up crying one night. Her mother ran into Linda's room to see what was wrong. "I was dreaming," sobbed Linda. "A monster was chasing me and I couldn't get away."

"Tell me about it," said her mother. Linda described the monster.

"There is no animal like that anywhere in the world, Linda. So go back to sleep and I'll see you in the morning." Linda felt better, but she still asked her mother to leave the hall light on — just in case!

 When Linda described the monster to her mother, she painted a word picture.

1. Can you draw Linda's monster? Use the word picture to help.

It was brown and hairy with six fingers. Each finger had a sharp claw on the end. Its body was round and fat, but it was very tall — taller than a giraffe and fatter than an elephant. On top of its ugly head it had a pointy horn. It had mean eyes and a long purple tongue. It was very angry. When it growled I could see several short, sharp, green fangs.

2. Draw a circle around the describing words that helped you.

 These words have a special name. They are called adjectives. Adjectives describe nouns.

Adjectives: ordering

You can see from Linda's description of her monster that adjectives can be put before a noun or after a noun.
She said, "It had mean, angry eyes." (The adjective is in front of the noun.)
She said, "It was very angry." (The adjective is after the noun.)

1. Look at Linda's description. Which adjectives are in front of a noun?

_____

2. Which adjectives are after a noun?

_____

3. Look at the pictures below. On another piece of paper, write as many adjectives for each picture as you can.

Adjectives can tell us about the size, shape, condition, age and color of the noun they describe.
Here is an example. The little boy was sitting in a big, square, battered, old, gray box.

size — shape — condition — age — color

4. Here are some nouns.

| an animal | a vehicle | a bird | a fruit | a baby | a book | a teacher |

Write three adjectives for each on the lines below.
Complete the rest on another piece of paper.

You are using a list of adjectives, so do not forget to use commas.
You do not need to use a comma between the last adjective and the noun.

(a) an animal _____

(b) a vehicle _____

(c) a teacher _____

When we compare two things we use special adjectives. These are called comparatives because we are comparing. Many comparatives are made by adding "-er" to the adjective. For example: fat — fatter, long — longer, dirty — dirtier, great — greater.

When we compare more than two things we also use special adjectives, called superlatives. Many superlatives are made by adding "-est" to the adjective. For example: fat — fattest, long — longest, dirty — dirtiest, great — greatest.

Compare the items in each picture. The first one has been done.

(a)	(b)
The gorilla is tall.	The rabbit is fat.
The elephant is taller.	
The giraffe is the tallest.	
(c)	(d)
A bike is fast.	Tom is strong.
(e)	(f)
A kitten is small.	This person is old.

1. Now you know what comparatives and superlatives are, complete this table.

	comparative	superlative
hot	*hotter*	*hottest*
thin		
smooth		
heavy		
pretty		
wet		
strong		
rich		
small		
naughty		
angry		
tough		

2. Look at the words you have used in the table and check your spelling. Can you make up at least two spelling rules?

_____

_____

_____

1. Read this short play with a friend.
   (a) Mark the adjectives that are comparatives with a red "C."
   (b) Mark those that are superlatives with a blue "S."

2. Compare your answers.

The Greatest Gift of All

Jane looked at her test paper and burst into tears. Jan, her best friend, ran up to her.

Jan: What's wrong Jane? You look so sad.

Jane: It's this test. My grade is worse than last time and I studied hard. I'm not as smart as you. I'm a failure.

Jan: No, you're not. You're smarter than Tom. Your grade is better than his. You're not the worst in the class.

Jane: It's all right for you, you're the neatest and brightest in the class. You're better than anyone.

Jan: Only in some things. You're the most reliable student in the class. That's why Miss Lim always chooses you. You're the quickest at offering to help anyone. That's more important.

Jane: Do you really think so?

Jan: Why do you think you're my best friend?

        Good friends are the greatest gift of all.

---

3. Some adjectives are different. Complete this table to see how.

	comparative	superlative
(a) expensive		
(b) beautiful		
(c) honest		
(d) good		
(e) useful		

Comparative and superlative adjectives that have three or more syllables are formed by adding "more" or "most" before the word. So are those that end with "–ful."

Verbs are "doing" or action words. The verbs used in reports are special.

1. Underline the verbs in this report. Some are used more than twice.

Mammals

This report is about mammals. Mammals are animals that feed their young on milk. The females make the milk, so their babies have to stay with them until they can find their own food. There are many kinds of mammals in the world. A human is a mammal.

Mammals are different sizes. Some, like whales, are very big. Others, like mice, are very small. A mammal has body hair or fur. For example, cats and dogs have fur, but babies only have a few hairs on their heads. A mammal has warm blood, so it can live in very hot as well as very cold climates.

Most mammals are land animals but some live in the sea. Whales, dolphins and seals are sea mammals. Other mammals live under the ground or in trees. The bat is the only mammal that can fly.

In Australia there are some very unusual mammals. There are mammals that lay eggs. The echidna and platypus are egg-laying mammals. There are mammals that have a special pouch in which they carry their babies. The female koala has a pouch. So does the female kangaroo.

Mammals are the smartest of all the animals.

2. Did you underline is/are and has/have? _____

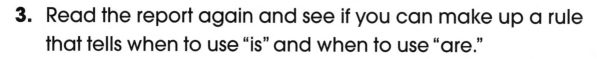 *These special verbs are used when you want to write about facts. Sometimes it is easy to make a mistake with these verbs.*

3. Read the report again and see if you can make up a rule that tells when to use "is" and when to use "are."

_____

_____

4. Now write a rule about when to use "has" and when to use "have."

_____

_____

Did you notice "is" and "has" are used when you talk about one person or thing and "are" and "have" are used when you talk about more than one person or thing?
There is one more tricky rule with these verbs — "are" and "have" are always used with the word "you." For example, "Have you brushed your teeth? Are you going to the movies with me? You are very lucky. You have to line up after recess."

1. Fill in the space with "has" or "have."

(a) The mailman _____ not been here yet.

(b) She _____ a big brother and a baby sister.

(c) The little boy _____ fallen into the pond.

(d) They _____ not answered my letter.

(e) One of the boys _____ taken my bike.

(f) Mom and Dad _____ promised to take me to the zoo.

(g) Monkeys _____ long tails and long arms.

2. Fill in the space with "is" or "are."

(a) An elephant _____ a mammal that lives in Africa and India.

(b) Dogs _____ carnivorous animals.

(c) Who _____ he going to choose for his partner?

(d) John and Mark _____ best friends.

(e) Who _____ you going to invite to your birthday party?

(f) The boys _____ sitting under the tree.

Verb tenses: tricky verbs

Some verbs are always used when telling about one person or thing.
For example: is, does, comes, gives, runs, was, goes.
Other verbs are used to tell about more than one person or thing.
For example: are, do, come, have, give, run, were, go.

1. **Read the sentences below and circle which word fits.**

    (a) He (go, goes) to the stores that (give, gives) the best prices.

    (b) The students (have, has) to (go, goes) to the teacher on duty.

    (c) I (run, runs) away when my sisters (is, are) chasing me.

    (d) Elephants (has, have) long trunks which (is, are) used to scoop up water.

    (e) My Mom and Dad (do, does) not like movies, but my sister (do, does).

    (f) The mailman, who (has, have) a motorbike, (come, comes) twice a day.

    (g) My dog (run, runs) to the gate when I (go, goes) for a walk.

    (h) You (is, are) not supposed to (give, gives) orders to me.

    (i) James (was, were) not in the playground with the children who (was, were) playing ball.

2. **Here is a short passage. It has 13 mistakes in it. Can you find and correct them? Write out your corrections. Write a happy ending.**

> Lee and vickie are twins there family are planning to have a party. their Mom and Dad goes to the store to order the cake. When the time come for the party to begin, the cake have not arrived. Everybody are worried. Many stores has already closed. Where was they going to get a cake.

1. Do you have a diary?   Yes ☐   No ☐

2. James gave Madison a diary for her birthday. She writes in her diary nearly every night. Read what she wrote about her school trip.

Our Trip to the Museum

Yesterday our class went to the museum. At 8:30 we **lined** up outside our classrooms and **walked** to the buses. On the way we sang songs. I sat next to Sarah.

When we **arrived** at the museum, Miss Lee **asked** us to find a partner. Of course Sarah was my partner. The museum guide **showed** us many interesting things. I **liked** the whale skeleton best. It was so big. Sarah liked the old-fashioned clothes. By then it was time for lunch, so we **walked** to a park near the museum. After lunch it was time to get back on the bus to go back to school.

We had a fun day at the museum. I hope I can go again. Grandpa will probably take me if I ask him.

---

3. Did you notice some of the verbs are in bold print? Write them in the spaces.

4. What is similar about these verbs? _____

_____

These verbs are written in the past tense. They tell us about something that has already happened. Diary writing (recount) has past tense verbs because you are writing about something that has already happened. Many past tense verbs are made by adding "-ed."

5. Here are some sentences that have the verb missing. Add a past tense verb to complete each.

(a) Mr. Lim _____ his hair before going out.

(b) The wolf _____ on the door of Grandma's house.

(c) The boy _____ up the ladder to the top.

Sometimes verbs can be very tricky. Some verbs change when you use them to talk about the past. Read the text below. It contains a tricky verb.

The principal was not very happy. His hands were quite sore. Every day he had to clap his hands loudly to tell the children that playtime and lunchtime were over. So he bought a new bell.

When it came time to go back into class, he brought out the new bell. The children were surprised. "Did you hear that?" said Albert. "Mr. Scott **runged** a bell."

"Yes," said his friend, "he **ranged** it very loudly."

"I think he **ringed** it to tell us to go back into class," said Brian.

1. What made the verb tricky? _____

_____

2. What verb should they have used? _____

3. Here are some sentences with the verbs missing.
Can you add the correct verb? Be careful. Some are tricky verbs.

(a) John likes to run. Yesterday he _____ to school.

(b) Birds always _____ to the tree near my bedroom

window. Yesterday, one _____ into my bedroom.

(c) Humpty Dumpty had a great _____.

He _____ off the wall.

(d) The choir can _____ many songs.

They _____ my favorite song this morning.

(e) All fish can _____. My fish _____ round and
round the pond yesterday.

Teachers Notes and Answers

Nursery Rhymes — Section 1

Page 10-50
This first section of *Grammar Skills* provides an introduction to language through a theme of Nursery Rhymes. Each Nursery Rhyme, as outlined in the Table of Contents (pages 4-5), has a detailed Teachers Notes section at the beginning of the activity pages. Answers for these pages are not provided.

Fairy Tales — Section 2

Page 51: Who is Speaking?
Question 2: Students examine the story of The Three Bears and the way their speech indicates their roles and relationships in the text. Did what they say show their age? Did words or punctuation (such as the exclamation mark) in the text tell us how the characters felt?
Question 2: "Someone's been sitting in my chair and I'm not happy!"
"Who's been eating my porridge?"
Question 3: "Someone's been sitting in my chair."
Question 4: Baby Bear — cry, looked up
Papa Bear — roared, shouted, not happy

Page 52: Add an Adverb
Discuss how some words add meaning to a verb. For example, "How am I running? I am running quickly." Answers will vary. Accept all answers that make sense.

Page 53: Exclamation Marks
Question 1: Someone's been sitting in my chair! Accept changes to the wording that makes the statement sound more aggressive.
Questions 2 and 3: Answers will vary.

Page 54: Looking at Connecting Words
Students look at how different ideas (clauses) in a sentence are joined with connecting words.
and, but, so, when, and

Page 55: Make it Connect
Answers will vary. Look at examples where connectives are used. Connectives are words which make the text flow from one sentence to another or from one sentence part to another.

Page 56: Storymap
Answers will vary.
Compare students' version of the story maps. Check that all major elements of the story have been included. Make a large class story map.

Page 57: Word Bank
Start a word bank for each student. Allow students to search for noun groups as the story is read and discussed. Word banks can be created for each story.

Page 58: Change the Mood of the Wolf
Answers will vary.
Look at traditional and contemporary version of the story and compare the language used.

Page 59: Using Words that Describe
Students use description to build noun groups. See how many ways they can describe the characters, for example, "the big wolf, the big hairy wolf, the ferocious hairy creature."

Questions 1 to 3: Answers will vary. Discuss and compare students' responses.
Question 4: house — brick, small; horse — fast, hungry, big; ocean — rough, blue, smooth; apple — red, shiny, crunchy.

Legends

Page 60: Character Profile
Read and discuss the legend of King Arthur. By developing a profile, students develop an understanding of how characters' actions and reactions form an important part of the legend. Answers will vary.

Page 61: King Arthur
Discuss the legend of King Arthur before completing the cloze activity.
Question 1: pulled, He, castle, Arthur, around, was. Accept all reasonable answers.
Question 2: Answers will vary.

Page 62: Cut and Sequence
King Arthur became king when he pulled the sword from the stone. King Arthur and the knights would sit around a great round table and plan their adventures.

Page 63: Cut and Sequence
Two duck sisters were waddling down the road to the pond for a swim.
On their way they met a fox sitting on a fence.
"Good morning, ladies," said the fox. "Are you on your way to the pond?"
"Oh yes, said the sisters, we come along here every day."
"Interesting," said the fox, with a toothy smile. "Have a nice swim."
The next morning the first sister said "I think we should take another road to the pond."
"No," said the second sister. "I am used to this road." So off they went along the same road.
Up ahead the fox was waiting and tried to catch the duck sisters. They were able to get away but decided they would not take the same road every time.

Page 64: Using Pronouns
Question 1: Possible use of pronouns: they, He, They, they, he, They, them.
Some pronouns can be replaced with names to stop overuse.
Question 2: Answers will vary.

Page 65: Talking Ducks
Students discuss what the ducks might be saying to each other.
Questions 1 to 3: Answers will vary. Discuss the placement of quotation marks around the part that is actually spoken.

Page 66: Cut and Sequence

The baboon was taking his daily walk in the jungle. He met his friend, the gibbon, on the path.

"My good friend," said the gibbon, "how strange to find you holding an open umbrella over your head on such a sunny day as this."

"Yes," said the baboon. "I am most annoyed. I can not lose this disagreeable umbrella. I am stuck. I would not think of walking without my umbrella in case it should rain."

"But, as you see, I am not able to enjoy the sunshine underneath this dark shadow. It is sad."

"There is a simple solution," said the gibbon. "You need only to cut some holes in your umbrella. Then the sun will shine on you."

"What a good idea!" The baboon went home and cut holes in his umbrella.

In the end the baboon got soaked to the skin.

Page 67: Procedure — Umbrella Repair

Answers will vary.
Check that procedures include all three parts.

Page 68: Search for Adjectives

Answers will vary. Use adjectives to make noun groups.

Myths

Cronos was ruler of heaven and Earth. He married Rhea and together they had three sons: Hades, Poseidon and Zeus and three daughters Demeter, Hestia and Hera.
Cronus did not trust his children because he had been told that a son of his would take over the throne. To stop this from happening he swallowed each child as it was born. Zeus was the last to be born. Rhea couldn't bear to see another of her children swallowed so she wrapped a stone in a blanket and gave it to Cronus telling him it was baby Zeus. Cronus believed Rhea and swallowed the stone. Rhea then took Zeus to a safe place where he grew up strong and tall.
Zeus met his first wife Metis and together they planned to free his brothers and sisters and take over his father's power. Metis secretly put something in Cronus' drink and it made him sick. He vomited up the stone and then Zeus' brothers and sisters. They were all ready to fight Cronus so he surrendered his powers.
Zeus became ruler of the sky and earth. He was forced to fight many battles with titans and giants and many fearsome creatures.
It was believed there was no one more powerful than Zeus.

Page 69: Zeus: Complete the Cloze

Question 1: was, the, thunderbolt, hurled, made, lied.
Question 2: Answers will vary.

Page 70: Zeus: Character Profile

Answers will vary.

Page 71: Processes for Zeus

Discuss the difference between mental processes and material processes. Brainstorm lists of each type of process.
Questions 1 to 3: Answers will vary.

Page 72: Compare Yourself to Zeus

Share answers with class.

Page 73: Animal Research

Gather mythological stories. Students choose a god and take notes from stories. Students write a report on a god.

Question 1: Make sure students have included all elements of a report.
Question 2: Answers will vary. Students read starters to class and discuss.

Section 3 — Grammar

Nouns

Stress the points listed below:
- nouns are naming words — they represent the names of persons, places or things;
- nouns that name things you can see and touch are called common nouns;
- some nouns are countable nouns because they can be made plural; for example, girl — girls;
- some nouns are uncountable nouns because they are always singular; e.g. rice can't be made plural by adding an s. You have to add something else to it, such as "three bags of" rice;
- nouns can be singular or plural.

Page 74: Identifying Common Nouns

Question 1: Nouns are naming words.
Question 2: cat, foot
Question 3: man/father, umbrella, boy, shell, water/beach/ocean, towel

Page 75: Classifying Common Nouns

Answers will vary.

Page 76: Plural Forms

Question 2: plural means more than one.
- the nouns in Row A (cows, bananas, and cars) are plurals made by adding an s;
- the nouns in Row B (teeth, feet, mice) all change form when they become plural;
- the nouns in Row C (deer, furniture, butter) don't change. They need other words to make them plural (two deer, three pieces of furniture, four boxes of butter).

Page 77: Plural Spelling Rules

Plural nouns can be made in a number of different ways. For example:
- add s to form the plural of most words;
- add es to form the plural of words ending in ch, sh, ss or x and some words ending in o;
- for nouns ending in y (preceded by a consonant) change the y to i and add es;
- for most nouns ending in fe or f, change these letters to ves;
- change the vowels of some sounds such as tooth — teeth;
- some words ending in o do not need an es.
Question 1: (a) girl, mountain, cat, hat (b) by adding "s" to the singular form.
Question 2: (a) beach, ash, bunch, brush, wish, box, branch, tax (b) by adding "es" to the singular
Question 3: (a) party, story, army (b) by changing the "y" to "i" and adding "ies."

Page 78: Irregular Plurals
Question 1: (a) teeth (b) men (c) geese (d) mice
(e) feet (f) women (g) children
Question 2: (a) few, many (b) cup of
Ask students to suggest different answers.
- uncountable nouns are always singular and are not used with articles such as a and an;
- some expressions of quantity such as: a lot of, plenty of, a little, much, some, any, large amounts of and a great deal of are used with uncountable nouns; and
- some expressions of quantity such as: a lot of, plenty of, any, some, many, a large number of and a few are used with countable nouns.
  Have students identify the expressions of quantity that can be used with both countable and uncountable nouns and those that only apply to one or the other.

Adverbs

Page 79: Telling How
Question 2: The words are all adverbs of manner — they tell "how."
Question 3: (a) tells how mother shook Madison (b) tells how the sun was shining (c) tells how father was waiting (d) tells how Madison climbed out of bed (e) tells how she dressed (f) tells how she ran down stairs.
Question 4: Answers will vary. Students share answers with the whole class. Make a chart of actions and adverbs that describe how.

Page 80: That Tell Frequency and Time
Question 2: one day, soon, all day, always, the next day, before, tomorrow, yesterday, today, earlier, always.
Question 3: Answers will vary.

Page 81: Identifying Adjectives
Question 2: The following words should be circled: brown, hairy, six, sharp, round, fat, tall, taller than, fatter than, ugly, pointy, mean, long, purple, angry, several, short, sharp, green.
Some adjectives are quantity adjectives. These can describe definite or indefinite quantities; e.g. two, many, double, third, several. Some adjectives can be comparative adjectives; e.g. fatter, taller.

Page 82: Ordering
Question 1: six, sharp, taller than, fatter than, ugly, pointy, mean, long, purple, several, short, sharp, green.
When adjectives are listed before a noun the usual order is: size (except for little) description, age (and the adjective little), shape, color, material, origin.

Page 83: Comparatives and Superlatives — 1
Question 1: (b) The cat is fatter. The pig is the fattest. (c) A train is faster. A plane is fastest. (d) Phil is stronger. Ed is the strongest. (e) A mouse is smaller. A fly is the smallest. (f) This person is older. This person is the oldest.
One or two-syllable adjectives form their comparatives and superlatives by adding er and est to the positive form; e.g. happy, happier, happiest. Adjectives with three or more syllables form their comparative and superlative by putting more and most before the positive; e.g. worried, more worried, most worried.
Some are irregular; e.g. bad, worse, worst; good, better, best; old, elder, eldest; much, more, most.

Page 84: Comparatives and Superlatives — 2
Question 2: All follow the one or two-syllable rule above. When adding the suffix er or est to words with a short vowel sound, you need to double the consonant to keep the vowel sound short; e.g. hot-hotter-hottest, thin-thinner-thinnest, wet-wetter-wettest. When adding the suffix er or est to a word ending in y change the y to i and add es; e.g. heavy – heavier – heaviest; pretty – prettier – prettiest; naughty – naughtier – naughtiest; angry – angrier – angriest.

Page 85: Comparatives and Superlatives — 3
Refer to the syllable rules shown for page 83.

Verb tenses

The report genre gives facts and information about a class of things. It uses timeless present tense because it refers to facts that are current.

Page 86: Timeless Present Tense — 1
Questions 1 and 2: Be sure that students identify is/are and has/have as verbs. Other verbs include: feed, make, find, live, fly, lay, carry.
Questions 3 and 4: The verbs is and has are used with singular nouns and the verbs are and have are used with plural nouns.

Page 87: Timeless Present Tense — 2
Question 1: (a) has (b) has (c) has (d) have (e) has (f) have (g) have
Explain that example (e) can be tricky. The subject of the sentence is one of the boys, therefore it is singular.
Question 2: (a) is (b) are (c) is (d) are (e) are (f) are
Explain that examples (c) and (e) are tricky. The subject of example (c) is he — he/she always use the auxiliary is/has. The subject of (e) is you — you/they/we always use the auxiliary are/have.

Page 88: Tricky Verbs
Question 1: (a) goes, give (b) have, go (c) run, are (d) have, are (e) do, does (f) has, comes (g) runs, go (h) are, give (i) was, were
Question 2: Lee and Vicki are twins. Their family is planning to have a party. Their Mom and Dad go to the store to order the cake. When the time comes for the party to begin, the cake has not arrived. Everybody is worried. Many stores have already closed.

Where are they going to get a cake?

Page 89: Past Tense
Question 3: Diary and journal entries are recounts. They are written in past tense because they tell about things that have already happened. All the verbs end in ed because they tell about something that has already happened.
Question 5: (a) brushed, combed (b) knocked, banged, rapped, hammered, tapped (c) climbed, clambered, struggled.
Have students offer as many different past tense verbs as they can to complete each sentence. Discuss whether each different verb changes the meaning of the sentence.

Page 90: Past Tenses and Irregular Verbs
Questions 1 and 2: The verb is tricky because it is not formed by adding an ed. The formation is irregular. The verb should have been rang.
Question 3: (a) ran (b) fly, flew (c) fall, fell (d) sing, sang (e) swim, swam

Quotation Marks

1. **Put quotation marks in the story.**

   Do you want to come on a magic carpet ride? asked the genie.

   Yes, please! shouted Trudy and Kirsty.

   We're going to a land far, far away, said genie dreamily.

   I hope that it's a friendly land, said Trudy.

   So do I, replied Kirsty.

   We will fly straight home if it's not, said

   the genie.

2. **Rewrite the story and put in the quotation marks. Each new speaker must begin on a new line.**

   I'm hot, said Karen.
   So am I, replied Paul.
   Let's go swimming, said Karen.
   All right! yelled Paul.
   Last one in is a rotten egg! yelled Karen.

_____

_____

_____

_____

_____

Looking for Spelling Errors

> It is important to spell correctly so we are able to read what has been written.

1. **Read the story carefully and put a circle around any words you think are wrong.** (Hint: There are four errors.)

   An apple is a froot. Apples are good to eat when thay

   are joocy and crisp. I like to take a brite red apple to school.

> A dictionary can be used to look up words that are spelled incorrectly. However, if the wrong letters are at the beginning of a word, it is difficult to find.
> Check the word by:
> - saying it slowly
> - listening carefully
> - stretching out the sounds
> - checking the first three letters.

2. **Write down the errors from the story.**
   Use a dictionary to check for the correct spelling.

   (a) _____   _____

   (b) _____   _____

   (c) _____   _____

   (d) _____   _____

3. **Read the story below and put a circle around any words you think are wrong.** (Hint: There are four errors.)
   Rewrite the sentence with the correct spelling.

   Yestaday I went to play in the parc.

   Dad halpt me to swing up hi.

   _____

   _____